Steve Austin
**The Story of the Wrestler
They Call "Stone Cold"**

**The Story of the Wrestler
They Call "Chyna"**

Mick Foley
**The Story of the Wrestler
They Call "Mankind"**

Ric Flair
**The Story of the Wrestler
They Call "The Nature Boy"**

Bill Goldberg

Billy Kidman

Brett Hart
**The Story of the Wrestler
They Call "The Hitman"**

**The Story of the Wrestler
They Call "Hollywood"
Hulk Hogan**

Lex Luger
**The Story of the Wrestler
They Call "The Total Package"**

Shawn Michaels
**The Story of the Wrestler
They Call "The Heartbreak Kid"**

Vince McMahon Jr.

Kevin Nash

**The Story of the Wrestler
They Call "Diamond"
Dallas Page**

Pro Wrestling: The Early Years

**Pro Wrestling's
Greatest Tag Teams**

**Pro Wrestling's
Greatest Matches**

Pro Wrestling's Greatest Wars

**Pro Wrestling's Most
Punishing Finishing Moves**

**The Story of the Wrestler
They Call "The Rock"**

Randy Savage
**They Story of the Wrestler
They Call "Macho Man"**

**They Story of the Wrestler
They Call "Sting"**

**They Story of the Wrestler
They Call "The Undertaker"**

Jesse Ventura
**They Story of the Wrestler
They Call "The Body"**

The Women of Pro Wrestling

CHELSEA HOUSE PUBLISHERS

The Story of the Wrestler
They Call "The Rock"

Dan Ross

Chelsea House Publishers
Philadelphia

Produced by Choptank Syndicate, Inc.

Editor and Picture Researcher: Mary Hull
Design and Production: Lisa Hochstein

CHELSEA HOUSE PUBLISHERS

Editor in Chief: Stephen Reginald
Production Manager: Pamela Loos
Art Director: Sara Davis
Director of Photography: Judy L. Hasday
Managing Editor: James D. Gallagher
Senior Production Editor: J. Christopher Higgins
Project Editor: Anne Hill
Cover Illustrator: Keith Trego

Cover Photos: Jeff Eisenberg Sports Photography

The Chelsea House World Wide Web site
address is http://www.chelseahouse.com

3 5 7 9 8 6 4 2

Library of Congress Cataloging-in-Publication Data

Ross, Dan
        The Rock: the story of the wrestler they call "the Rock" / by Dan Ross
            p.   cm.— (Pro wrestling legends)
        Includes bibliographical references and index.
        Summary: A biography of the wrestler Rocky Maivia, known as "the Rock."
        ISBN 0-7910-5831-X — ISBN 0-7910-5832-8 (pbk.)
        1. Rock (Wrestler) —Juvenile literature. 2. Wrestlers—United States—
Biography—Juvenile Literature. [1. Rock (Wrestler) . 2. Wrestlers. 3. Samoan
Americans—Biography] I. Title. II. Series.

    GV1196.R63 R67 2000
    796.812'092— dc21
    [B]
                                                            00-021865

Contents

1 KING OF ALL MANKIND

For some wrestlers, it all begins and ends with the fans. But Rocky Maivia had to wonder what the fans had ever done for him. How had they ever helped him accomplish anything in his career?

One thing he would always remember was the night in 1997, when, for no reason at all, the fans started chanting, "Rocky Sucks!" and "Rocky Die!" Rocky Maivia had been perfectly willing to toe the company line, to do things the so-called "right way," but still the fans had turned against him.

It was all because he had tried to convince his father, former wrestling champion Rocky Johnson, that he was doing something good. He told him that he was doing the right thing by joining the group of rulebreakers called the Nation of Domination. At first, his father was dismayed, but before long he came around to Maivia's way of thinking, and realized that the fans couldn't do anything for his son.

"That's my son!" Johnson boasted after watching Rocky Maivia pretend to be beaten, then get up from playing possum to beat Hunter Hearst Helmsley, also known as Triple-H. "Wrestling's a sport of cunning, not just physical contact. Everyone's in awe of my son's great physique and conditioning, but he also has the intelligence to put it all together. I taught

When wrestling fans turned against the Rock, he told them he didn't care what they thought.

him that old possum trick years ago. I'm surprised he still remembered it."

Now, on the biggest and most important stage of his life, the World Wrestling Federation (WWF) Survivor Series on November 15, 1998, Rocky Maivia was about to unveil a new version of the possum trick, a version he hadn't learned from his father, but rather created for himself: trick

Hunter Hearst Helmsley's body-guard, Chyna, managed to protect him from the Rock while he and Maivia were feuding.

your friends, trick the fans, trick the world, and leave everyone wondering what hit them.

The summer before, Maivia had emerged as the leader of the Nation of Domination, and had become embroiled in a heated feud with Hunter Hearst Helmsley. Maivia was the Intercontinental champion. Because of his feud with Helmsley, he was also a fan favorite. The only thing that kept him from squashing Helmsley on a regular basis was Helmsley's bodyguard, Chyna, who kept interfering on Triple-H's behalf.

At SummerSlam '98, Maivia had lost the Intercontinental title to Helmsley in a spectacular ladder match. Maivia was crushed by the defeat, but rather than set his sights on regaining the belt from his hated rival, he aimed at a bigger goal: the WWF World heavyweight title held by "Stone Cold" Steve Austin.

At the time, Austin and Maivia weren't exactly close friends, but they got along well enough. They shared a mutual hatred for Vince McMahon Jr., the megalomaniac owner of the WWF, and teamed several times against The Undertaker and Kane, who had been doing McMahon's dirty work for him inside the ring, and sometimes in the locker rooms. Occasionally, Maivia was able to secure a match against Austin for the World title, but he was never able to beat him.

"He [Austin] was very influential on the Rock, and at times he still can be, make no mistake about it," Maivia told WWF *Raw* magazine. "When we go out there and get in that ring, something special happens. When it's right, something special happens and fireworks happen. And when it's the Rock and Stone Cold and we're doing our thing, with all the emotion set in, it's a heck of a match. But at the same time, I do respect him. I respect him in every way possible. He's a heck of a champion. But at the same time, when the time is right I'll take the belt off Steve Austin. And he's gonna take the 'Rock Bottom,' and he's gonna take it right in the middle of the ring, 1-2-3."

Maivia, however, didn't get the chance to face Austin. On September 27, 1998, Austin lost the World title in a triple-threat match when he was simultaneously pinned by The Undertaker and Kane. The title was declared vacant, and a 14-man tournament for the championship was scheduled for the 1998 Survivor Series. Maivia planned to be there, along with 13 of the other top wrestlers in the federation.

Maivia was confident he would emerge from the Survivor Series as champion, not simply because he was always confident, but because he had fond memories of other Survivor Series in which he had wrestled. He had, in fact, made his WWF debut at the 1996 Survivor Series, where he teamed with Marc Mero, Barry Windham, and Jake Roberts to defeat Goldust, Helmsley, Jerry Lawler, and Crush. The Rock was the last man standing in that elimination match.

Now, with another Survivor Series looming, the 6' 5", 275-pound former college football star was ready to fulfill the destiny he had chosen for himself, a destiny his father and his grand-father, legendary wrestler Peter Maivia, had never been able to fulfill: to become a world champion. This was a goal the Rock never doubted he could achieve.

"When the character started developing, I went to Vince McMahon and told him that I saw the Rock as the new millennium version of Ric

Flair," Maivia said. "He wears $500 shirts. The Rock's a little more brash. The great thing about the Rock is there's a lot of depth. In the Rock's eyes, he's the smartest guy walking God's green earth. He's extremely intelligent and cocky."

The Rock had realized a year earlier, when he wrested control of the Nation of Domination from Faarooq, that if he wanted something, he had to take it. He would walk into the Kiel Center in St. Louis and grab with both hands.

Round one of the Survivor Series brought no surprises. Mankind, Steve Austin, and Ken

Mankind applies his mandible claw maneuver on the Rock while Kane prepares to stomp a prone Steve Austin.

Shamrock, three of the favorites in the tournament, won their matches. So did Maivia, who caught a lucky break. He had been scheduled to face Helmsley, but Helmsley injured his knee and was replaced by the less-imposing Big Bossman. Maivia beat him in only four seconds.

As the evening wore on, it became clear that there was some kind of conspiracy between Maivia and McMahon. Bossman had been a plant by McMahon, sent into the tournament to lay down for Maivia. Later, Bossman and McMahon's henchmen, Pat Patterson and WWF Commissioner Sergeant Slaughter, harassed Maivia's opponents. The Rock defeated Shamrock in the quarterfinals. In the semifinals, he defeated The Undertaker, setting up a championship showdown with Mankind.

McMahon hated Mankind, and there was no way he was going to allow him to become WWF World champion. How far would McMahon go to ensure victory for the Rock? As far as he had to. When the Rock caught Mankind in a sharpshooter, a leglock in which the protagonist places extreme pressure on the victim's thighs and lower back, McMahon ran to ringside and called for the timekeeper to ring the bell, signaling Mankind's submission and defeat.

Mankind claimed he had never submitted. Indeed, videotape replays showed that Mankind never motioned with his hands or with his mouth that he wanted to give in. Later, Mankind would declare that there was no way he would have ever submitted to Maivia.

It didn't matter. McMahon ran the show and he wanted the Rock to be WWF World champion. The Rock was now on top, and he embraced

McMahon. "Kiss my butt," he told the fans, whose boos nearly drowned him out.

Austin ran into the ring and attacked Maivia and McMahon, but Maivia didn't really care. "There's only one person who hates the fans more than the McMahons, and that's the Rock," Maivia said shortly after the victory. "We couldn't wait to lay the smack down on them. Now Mr. McMahon has a champion he can be proud of—the best World champion the WWF ever had."

The possum trick had worked its magic. It wasn't the first time, and it certainly wouldn't be the last.

2 IT RUNS IN THE FAMILY

From the day he was born—May 2, 1972—there was never any doubt that Duane Johnson would one day become a professional wrestler. Duane's grandfather, High Chief Peter Maivia, was one of the first Samoan professional wrestlers, and to this day is acknowledged as a genuine wrestling legend. Duane's father, Rocky Johnson, was one of the most popular wrestlers in North America during the 1970s, and in 1983 he joined forces with Tony Atlas to win the WWF World tag team title. His uncle, Jimmy Snuka, was one of the most popular wrestlers in the world in the early and mid-1980s and a top contender for the WWF World heavyweight title, then held by Bob Backlund. Two other uncles wrestled as the Samoans, and won the WWF World tag team title several times. Even Duane's mother, Ata, once aspired to become a pro wrestler.

"Wrestling is in the blood," Duane said. "It never leaves." The Rock—Rocky Maivia—would need 24 years to find out just how right he was.

Duane Johnson had an unusual childhood. Unlike most wrestling families, the Johnsons went wherever Rocky went, and Rocky Johnson ended up in a lot of places: Hawaii, where Duane spent most of his formative years, Florida, Georgia,

Growing up in a wrestling family, Duane Johnson traveled extensively, living in places like Hawaii, Florida, Georgia, and New Zealand.

The Rock took his name from Don "the Rock" Muraco, who was the chief rival of Duane's father, Samoan wrestler High Chief Peter Maivia.

and even New Zealand. Like a child born into a military family, Duane got used to the traveling life very quickly. The Johnsons lived in 15 states and several countries. Duane thought nothing of meeting wrestling legends such as Andre the Giant and Freddie Blassie.

At night, Duane got to watch his father hold a crowd in the palm of his hand and beat some of the top wrestlers of his day. Ironically, one of Rocky Johnson's most hated rivals, Don Muraco, was nicknamed "the Rock."

It was a life filled with travel, loving parents, exciting nights, and meals with the family. Duane never lacked for attention, and when he had some free time, he'd try out some of the moves he had learned from his father: a headlock here, an armlock there, an occasional elbowdrop and once in a rare while, maybe even a piledriver. Father and son loved to play around in the practice ring.

The older he got, the more Duane got into wrestling. He rented every wrestling video he could get his hands on. He didn't merely watch them, he examined them like a scientist, studying and memorizing them. His grandfather's dreams, his father's dreams, his uncles' dreams—they had all become his dreams, too. Their reality would become his reality.

Despite his unorthodox childhood, Duane was disciplined and focused. He rarely missed school, his grades were good, and his parents taught him proper morals. Rocky Johnson passed his work ethic on to his son. The Johnsons were never rich, and they rarely had extra money for real luxuries, but they were always happy. They were a solid family in every way.

When Duane was a teenager, the Johnsons' travels brought them to Allentown, Pennsylvania. As a sophomore at Freedom High School, Duane still had no doubt that he wanted to become a pro wrestler. He had been training with his father since the day he was born, and training seriously since he was 14.

"I grew up in the business, was kept close to the business, and was never sheltered from it," Johnson told the *Wisconsin State Journal*.

Even at 16, Duane was big and strong. He was 6' 5", 242 pounds, and could bench-press over 400 pounds. He was hard to miss walking down the halls, and it wasn't surprising when the football coach at Freedom High noticed him. When Duane was a junior, he joined the high school football team.

At the start, Duane knew next to nothing about football. He was a fast learner, however, and his size and athletic ability made him an imposing player. One year later, *USA Today* rated him the eighth-best player in Pennsylvania, one of the best states for high school football in the entire country. As a senior, Duane received letters from nearly 500 colleges and was heavily recruited by Penn State, UCLA, and the University of Miami, all college football powerhouses. Duane was on the verge of becoming the first member of his family to go against the wrestling grain.

"Uncles, grandfathers, cousins. When they come to visit, that's all we ever talk about is wrestling," Rocky Johnson told the *Miami Herald*. "They were pushing him a little bit. They'd tell him, 'When you get into wrestling, you're gong to be a big star.' I wanted him to make up his own mind. I tried to help him. I could see he was really serious about football."

This wasn't an easy decision. As a pro wrestler, Duane could have started making big money immediately. As a college football player, he'd have to settle for the cheers of the fans and pats on the back from his teammates. No money, just a chance at glory.

Duane ultimately accepted a full scholarship to play defensive tackle for the University of Miami Hurricanes under coach Dennis Erickson. At first, Duane had a hard time fitting in because of his lack of football experience.

"He wasn't football smart," said former Hurricanes defensive coordinator Tommy Tuberville. "There's a big difference between wrestling and football. It's not a big, bulky game. He was more of a bodybuilder guy."

Duane couldn't deny his heritage. K.C. Jones, who would go on to play for the Denver Broncos of the National Football League (NFL), was Johnson's teammate from 1992 to 1994, and recalled a guy who just couldn't stop wrestling. "He was a good defensive tackle, but wrestling was in his blood," Jones told the *Rocky Mountain News*. "He had the build and the family background. You can definitely tell that he had the charisma. He's really a great guy, funny, and laid-back."

Although Johnson started only one of 39 games in his four years at Miami, he was on a national championship team in 1991 and made a lot of tackles in his final two years. He was a pre-season All-American prior to his senior year and had a chance of being drafted by an NFL team. Early in the 1994 season, however, Johnson suffered two ruptured disks in his back. Instead of undergoing surgery, he decided to fight through the pain and complete the season. Often, he was in agony. The pain was excruciating. He stood in the aisles on the team's flights home because he couldn't sit down. Somehow, he finished the season, but his subpar play—only 8 solo tackles after making 15 the year before—ruined his hopes of getting drafted.

Among the legendary wrestlers in Duane Johnson's family is Jimmy "Superfly" Snuka, who is Duane's uncle.

He graduated from Miami in 1995 with degrees in criminology and exercise management. His grades put him in the top 10 percent of his class."Being a student-athlete taught me about dedication and sacrifice and time management," he told the *Wisconsin State Journal.* "It taught me all about the little things I need to know now to be the best that I can be."

As expected, the NFL never came calling, so Johnson signed a three-year contract with the Calgary Stampeders of the Canadian Football League. Wrestling would have to wait. Unfortunately, glory wasn't waiting for Duane in the CFL. The weather was freezing. His salary was just $400 a week. He was sitting on the bench, hardly playing. He began to realize that it was time to go back to wrestling.

When the season ended, he got in his car, drove home, and moved back into his parents' house in Tampa. He reached into his pocket, saw that he had seven dollars to his name and quickly realized that no matter where he went, no matter what he did, he always had two things: supportive parents and the ability to wrestle.

Shortly after returning home, Duane called his football coach in Calgary and said, "Thanks for the one year. I'll pass on the final two years of my contract." Duane's football career was over.

Wrestling had taken a back seat in Duane's life for seven years, but now it was about to move back into the forefront. His father was happy to train him. They woke up at 6:00 each morning and worked together for three hours. At 9:00, Duane went to work as a personal trainer, a job that allowed him to lift weights when the gym wasn't busy. At night, Duane trained again with his father. It was an exhausting life, but Duane knew he would have to work especially hard to achieve his goal of becoming a superstar of the ring.

"I was like the dummy, the beat-up guy, which wasn't too much fun," Johnson told the *Miami Herald*. "I was the guy who got body-slammed and piledrived. Nobody likes to get bodyslammed or piledrived. But it's like football practice. It's all for the cause."

On weekends, when Duane wasn't wrestling, he would receive a dawn-to-dusk lesson in wrestling from his father. Finally, he got his first big opportunity. In March 1996, Duane traveled to Corpus Christi, Texas, where he had secured a tryout with the WWF. He'd landed a match against Steve Lombardi, who was known as the "Brooklyn Brawler." Duane won. The WWF people were impressed, but they wanted to see more.

Duane was happy to oblige. This time, he was going to make the most of his opportunity.

I n wrestling, as in any professional sport, having a well-known name or a famous father is like having a backstage pass to a concert. Rocky Johnson was able to open some doors for his son, but now Duane had to prove that he was worthy of the opportunity he had been given.

When WWF promoters suggested that Duane get more experience before trying to compete against the formidable competition in the high-profile organization, he signed with a federation located in Tennessee called the United States Wrestling Association (USWA). While not as large a promotion as the WWF, the USWA was no small-time outfit. Its top star was Jerry "the King" Lawler, one of the most famous wrestlers in the world. Another top USWA wrestler at the time was Jeff Jarrett, who would later wrestle in both the WWF and World Championship Wrestling (WCW). The USWA was one of the top independent federations in the United States and just a half-step away from the big time.

This was an outstanding place for Duane to get additional experience. Oddly, however, when he made his USWA debut on June 2, 1996, in Cookeville, Tennessee, Duane had ditched his famous last name for a more colorful ring name: Flex Kavana. The name was appropriate, considering his muscular build and

Making his WWF debut at Madison Square Garden in a Survivor Series-style match on November 17, 1996, Rocky Maivia prepares to pin Goldust.

dark skin, but it was hardly the kind of name that would get him taken seriously.

The fact was, however, that Duane Johnson didn't want to be known for his name. He didn't want people to say, "Oh, that kid is Rocky Johnson's son." He didn't want to prosper from his father's name and reputation. If he got something, he wanted it to be because he earned it.

Flex Kavana defeated the Punisher in his first match. A few days later, he beat Tony Falk. The Punisher and Falk were not title contenders, but Kavana had soundly beaten them and the victories counted.

He got his first big break on June 17, 1996, in a one-night tournament for the vacant USWA tag team title. Kavana's partner was Buzz Sawyer, a tough, wily veteran who had survived some of wrestling's greatest wars. In the first round, they defeated Falk and the Punisher. After receiving a second-round bye, Sawyer and Kavana defeated Brickhouse Brown and Reggie B. Fine in the finals. They won. Less than a month after making his pro debut, Duane Johnson had his first major title.

Sawyer and Kavana held the title for less than a month before losing the belts to the veteran Memphis duo of Jerry Lawler and Bill Dundee. However, people were already paying attention to the kid known as Flex Kavana. They took notice again when Kavana and Sawyer regained the belts a week later.

During these weeks in the USWA, Flex Kavana made no mention of his father, his grandfather, or his extensive wrestling background. Certainly, he thought about them every day and every time he stepped into the ring. He

In his WWF tryout, Rocky Maivia wrestled the late Owen Hart, who was impressed with his abilities and recommended that the WWF sign him.

had almost daily contact with his father. But as far as the rest of the wrestling world was concerned, Kavana was just some kid fresh out of the gym looking to catch his big break.

Kavana and Sawyer lost the belts for the final time on July 15, and Kavana turned his attention to singles competition. Although he rarely lost, he never got the chance to wrestle against the title holders. His career seemed to have stalled. Then, in the fall of 1996, the WWF came calling again.

This time, Duane's WWF tryout consisted of more than one match. He wrestled David Haskins at a *Monday Night Raw* taping and beat him. The next night, he lost to Owen Hart, the best wrestler he had faced during his short pro career. The loss might have been the most important match of Duane's career up until that time, because Owen was reporting back to his bosses in the WWF.

"He's better than half the guys you've got in the ring right now," Hart told WWF executives, according to *The Wrestler* magazine.

The WWF signed him for a few more matches, and he was impressive enough to be offered his first WWF contract in October 1996.

The Rock won his first title with Buzz Sawyer while he was tag team wrestling in the USWA under the name Flex Kavana.

Before Duane could step into the ring, the WWF had to take care of some important business: his ring name. He no longer wanted to be Flex Kavana. He didn't want to be Duane Johnson; that was too bland. Then the WWF suggested the name Rocky Maivia in honor of his father and grandfather. Duane balked. "No way!" he said. This was the same dilemma he had faced before: he didn't want to capitalize on his father's and grandfather's fame.

"Think about it," WWF officials told him. He went home and discussed the matter with his girlfriend, Dany. Finally, he came around to the WWF's way of thinking: Rocky Maivia it would be, as long as he wasn't billed as a carbon copy of his father and grandfather.

Rocky Maivia made his WWF debut in the 1996 Survivor Series pay-per-view on November 17 at Madison Square Garden, the world's most famous arena. Maivia was paired with Marc Mero, Barry Windham, and Jake Roberts in a Survivor Series-style match against Goldust, WWF Intercontinental champion Hunter Hearst Helmsley, Jerry Lawler, and Crush. In a Survivor Series match, the object is to eliminate each opponent on the opposing team by pinfall or submission, until all of the members of one team have been eliminated.

There were nearly 20,000 fans in the building that night. Very few of them had ever heard of Rocky Maivia. Chances are, none of them had ever seen him wrestle. By the time the night was over, however, every fan in the building knew exactly who Rocky Maivia was.

Roberts started the match by pinning Lawler. When Goldust pinned Windham, each side had three members remaining. Mero

Jerry "the King" Lawler was the star of the USWA when Duane Johnson began wrestling in that federation under the name Flex Kavana.

pinned Helmsley. Crush pinned Roberts. Each side was down to two members. Maivia was still standing. Then he got down to business. Maivia pinned Crush, then he pinned Goldust to win the bout for his team. It was as impressive a WWF debut as any wrestler in history had ever made.

Duane Johnson had walked into the spotlight as Rocky Maivia, and walked out as the WWF's newest rising star.

The fans loved him. "Rocky! Rocky!" they chanted whenever he stepped into the ring.

With his good looks, great physique, and charismatic personality, Maivia was an instant star. He piled up one victory after another, mostly over mid-level competition. When the year ended, Rocky finished third in the balloting for *Pro Wrestling Illustrated's* Rookie of the Year, an incredible accomplishment considering that he hadn't made his WWF debut until November.

Like the Rocky of movie fame who went from the gutter to glory, this latest Rocky of the ring had, in one year, gone from being a guy with seven dollars in his pocket to one with the world at his feet. In his own mind, though, Rocky Maivia knew he still had a long way to go, but he was determined to get there.

A TRIBUTE IN NAME ONLY

R ocky Maivia was far from being a contender for the WWF World title in January 1997. He had entered the federation only a few months earlier, and his biggest victory was still his first victory: the win for his team in the 1996 Survivor Series. But the Royal Rumble was one of wrestling's most unusual events, giving any 30 wrestlers the right to dream of securing a title shot at becoming the WWF World champion at WrestleMania. Even though Maivia wasn't ranked in the WWF Top 10, he stepped into the ring at the Royal Rumble on January 19, 1997, in San Antonio, Texas, intent on winning the bout, or at least making sure people remembered his performance at the Alamo Dome.

Under the rules of the Royal Rumble, the wrestlers enter the ring one at a time every minute. The only way to eliminate a wrestler is by dumping him over the top rope onto the arena floor. The last man standing is the winner, and the number one contender for the WWF World title.

With 48 minutes gone in the Royal Rumble, only six men remained in the ring: Maivia, Mankind, Terry Funk, The Undertaker, Steve Austin, and Bret Hart. Two of those men, Undertaker and Hart, were former WWF World champions. Funk was a legendary brawler. Austin was a top contender for

---

At age 24, the Rock became the youngest Intercontinental champion in WWF history when he wrestled the title away from Hunter Hearst Helmsley on February 16, 1997.

the WWF Intercontinental title. Meanwhile, Maivia had been wrestling for less than a year. He was in elite company.

Maivia's run ended 25 seconds after the 48-minute mark, when Mankind dumped him over the top. But once again, he had made an impact. He had gotten himself noticed, and not just because of his famous name.

There were times during the first month and a half of 1997 that Maivia really struggled. He beat the low-in-the-card guys, like Salvatore Sincere and Leif Cassidy, but had mixed results against Savio Vega, a member of the feared clique known as the Nation of Domination. The road to the top was long and hard, and he tried not to get discouraged.

On February 16, 1997, Maivia got the chance of his lifetime at the WWF's In Your House pay-per-view in Chattanooga, Tennessee. His opponent that night was Hunter Hearst Helmsley, the WWF Intercontinental champion. Helmsley was a big, strong wrestler who had been in the ring for five years and had been Intercontinental champion for over three months. By comparison, Maivia was just another up-and-coming grappler.

In one of the greatest upsets in the history of the Intercontinental title, Maivia scored a stunning victory to win the belt. Not only was he the Intercontinental champion, but, at age 24, he was the youngest Intercontinental champion in history.

Even his father had never won such a prestigious singles title. Suddenly, Maivia was one of the most famous wrestlers in the world. Helmsley said the victory was nothing but a fluke, but Maivia proved him wrong by beating him a second time only three days later. He continued to impress the wrestling world as he defeated Bret Hart, a former WWF World champion, to retain his belt.

Rocky took himself and the title center stage at WrestleMania XIII, the most important supercard of the year. His father was in his corner and watched closely as Rocky took a lot of punishment from the Sultan, but won anyway. The crowd chanted "Rocky! Rocky!" Their chants were louder than ever before. Rocky Maivia was on top of the world.

Unfortunately, the good times didn't last long. On April 28, 1997, Rocky lost the Intercontinental title to the man who had given him such a strong recommendation to the WWF in the first place—Owen Hart. The victory was decisive and by a clean pinfall. At the In Your House XV pay-per-view card in May, Rocky submitted to Mankind's mandible claw, a submission hold in which Mankind cut off the flow of air through Maivia's windpipe. The losses piled up. Before long, the fans turned against Maivia.

It was a stunning change in attitude, almost vicious in nature, on the part of the fans. They started chanting "Die, Rocky, Die!" and holding up signs that were grossly insulting. Maivia couldn't understand why the fans were booing him. He didn't think he had done anything wrong. All he had done was take advantage of the opportunities that had been accorded him. Rocky was furious. He couldn't understand why the fans hated him so much. For months, they had been part of his driving force, the reason why he wanted so desperately to succeed. "When all those fans get behind me, I think about the men who made me what

Nation of Domination leader Farooq was Maivia's rival on the football field and in pro wrestling.

I am today," he had said. "I can come back from anything."

Years later, he tried to put into words the way he felt during his first six months in the WWF and why the fans had turned against him. "Getting the belt way too early," Maivia told *WWF Magazine.* "Getting the push way too early. Being jammed down those people's throats way too early. [I was] a little apprehensive because of that, and it near killed me. It near pushed me over the edge."

This should have been a great time in Maivia's life. Despite the loss to Owen Hart, his career was taking off. Few wrestlers have won a major title in their rookie year, and Maivia was one of them. On May 3, 1997, he married Dany, his longtime girlfriend. He was impressing a lot of people, including his uncle, the great wrestler Jimmy Snuka.

"I keep tabs on all the newcomers, but Rocky is a very special person to me," Snuka told *Pro Wrestling Illustrated* magazine. "I was a contemporary of both his father and grand-father, and I knew them well, in and out of the ring. He's stronger and just as clever as any of us. It's like Rocky went to something like a wrestling smorgasbord, you know what I mean? He took his tray and said, 'I want some of Grandpop's karate kicks and chops, then I want some of Dad's quick punches. Oh, while I'm here, I'll take Jimmy Snuka's "Superfly" dive.' Man, that's some kind of package. The High Chief [Peter Maivia] would be proud."

Rocky Maivia was proud, but he was also humble and down to earth. He didn't think he was the greatest thing ever to enter a wrestling ring. He merely considered himself to be a hard-working young man who wanted to follow in his family's footsteps of greatness.

Meanwhile, a group of wrestlers calling them-selves the Nation of Domination was terrorizing the WWF. The group was led by Faarooq, who went by his real name, Ron Simmons, when he was WCW World champion and when he had played college football at Florida State University. The group also included Ahmed Johnson and D-Lo Brown, all minority wrestlers like Maivia, and rumors were circulating that they wanted

Afa, part of the tag team known as the Samoans, was Rocky Maivia's uncle. Since so many of his family members were wrestlers, the Rock was able to learn the techniques he admired from his father, grandfather, and uncles, and then incorporate them all to his advantage.

Maivia to join their clique. Maivia had already had some run-ins with the Nation. He had helped Ahmed Johnson against the Nation, only to have Johnson turn against him and join the group.

Maivia suffered another setback when he injured his right knee, forcing him out of action for three months. When he returned to the ring in mid-summer, he continued his battle with the Nation. One of his most interesting matches took place in Miami against Faarooq. This match was billed by the South Florida media as a showdown between Miami and Florida State University, because Maivia played football at Miami and Faarooq played football at Florida State (FSU), Miami's bitter rival.

"I'd do anything to win that match against Faarooq," Maivia said. "I remember along with 60 other teammates busting our butts for two weeks for the FSU game, working out a lot of hours. This match reminds me of all that. That was the game. That was the season. If we won, we'd probably be playing for the national title."

With no national title but a lot of pride at stake, Maivia defeated Faarooq, just as Miami had beaten FSU.

But Maivia had a lot of things on his mind, things more important than reviving football rivalries. Suddenly, joining the Nation seemed appealing, but he didn't know what to do. His father and grandfather had never been rule-breakers. He had always been taught to do the right thing. But where had doing things right gotten him so far? The fans were booing him, and he wasn't getting the title shots he felt he deserved.

The time had come for Maivia to make some difficult decisions that could change his life.

5 DOMINATION

Rocky Johnson didn't want Rocky Maivia to join the Nation of Domination. He couldn't understand why his son would want to side with such a nefarious group of rulebreakers, men who seemingly had no interest in doing things the right way and obviously had no respect for anyone who wasn't a member of their clique. Rocky Johnson talked to his son on the telephone. He tried to make him see things his way.

But Rocky Maivia no longer knew what to do. He tried to think of reasons why he shouldn't join the Nation of Domination.

On August 11, 1997, Faarooq was wrestling Chainz on a television broadcast of *Raw Is War*. The referee got knocked out during the contest. When Chainz tried to pin Faarooq, Maivia entered the ring and choke-slammed Chainz. As simply as that, Maivia was a member of the Nation of Domination.

"What was the use?" Maivia said, explaining his turn. "They [the fans] didn't like me then, they're sure not going to like me now."

While wrestling fans continued to boo Maivia and the wrestling world was taken aback by his arrogance, Rocky's father finally came around to his son's way of thinking. Finally, he approved of him joining the Nation of Domination.

WWF Intercontinental champion Steve Austin used his "Stone Cold stunner" to defeat the Rock at the D-Generation X pay-per-view on December 7, 1997.

"The fans had no right to boo my son whenever he was in the ring," Rocky Johnson said. "He was fighting for them. Now I see his confidence improving because he's with a group of winners. He doesn't need the fans at all."

At the Badd Blood pay-per-view in October, Maivia teamed with fellow Nation members Kama Mustafa and D-Lo Brown to defeat the Road Warriors, former WWF and WCW World tag team champions. Although Maivia sacrificed most of his singles wrestling career for the good of the Nation, it was clear that he was improving as a wrestler and, as his father had said, gaining confidence.

In fact, he was doing more than gaining confidence. His entire ring personality was changing. He started calling himself the Rock and always referred to himself in the third person, beginning each utterance with the phrase, "the Rock says . . ." He insulted the fans. He insulted his opponents. He was ruthless. He even insulted the homeless, saying things like, "Stay off the Rock's finely manicured lawn." He wore expensive watches and clothes. The Rock was no longer a man of the people.

The Nation of Domination continued its reign of terror over the WWF, with Faarooq and Maivia leading the charge. One of their primary targets was Intercontinental champion "Stone Cold" Steve Austin, whom Maivia faced in a title match at the D-Generation X pay-per-view on December 7, 1997, in Springfield, Massachusetts.

Like Maivia, Austin was a bit of a renegade. The difference, however, was that the fans liked Stone Cold, a tough guy with an attitude. For this match, he drove his truck to ringside. Before the night was over, Austin had executed his signature move, the Stone Cold stunner, to Nation member D-Lo Brown—on top of the truck. He also used his "stunner" to defeat Maivia.

Maivia was enraged over Austin's actions. WWF head Vince McMahon Jr. was, too. The next night at *Raw Is War*, McMahon told Austin that he was not happy to see him use the truck as a weapon. He ordered a rematch on the spot. Austin, however, wasn't going to be told what to do or whom to wrestle. Rather than put his belt on the line once again, he simply handed the belt to McMahon. Then he executed another "stunner" on McMahon, grabbed the belt, and threw it in a nearby river.

McMahon accepted Austin's title resignation, and awarded the belt to Maivia, who suddenly— and without stepping into the ring or defeating the former champion—was the new Inter- continental champ. Maivia was making no apolo- gies for how he "won" the belt for the second time.

"Hey, is it my fault that Austin was afraid to get into the ring with me again?" Maivia said in an interview with *The Wrestler* magazine. "Is it my fault that he was afraid to deal with the Nation of Domination? No. Austin had the belt. It meant a lot to him. He wasn't going to give it up for nothing. But it was probably a smart decision considering the shape his spine is in. The Rock could have done serious damage to that neck of his. He gave up the title to me rather than lose it in the ring, which is exactly what would have happened. He knew it, I knew it, everybody knew it. Austin's a coward. He'll come out there with his big truck, or he'll attack the Rock from behind, but when it came to a face-to-face match, he wanted no part of that. Where's his guts?"

The way Maivia became champion made the fans hate him even more. He didn't care. He called the fans "weak and pathetic." He scolded them for not realizing he was a great athlete. Besides, he figured, even though they hated him, they were paying attention to him. The Rock was making headlines. He was big news.

"I can think specifically about autograph sessions that I would go to thinking to myself, 'Man, these people really hate me,' because people were buying 'Rocky Sucks' T-shirts," Maivia told *WWF Magazine.* "So, for somebody to spend $25 for a T-shirt that says 'Rocky Sucks,' there really has to be a lot of hatred there for some reason. So I'm thinking if these people really hate me, I'm wondering if people are actually gonna want my autograph. And then I go to the autograph sessions and there's near 1,000 people at them!"

Maivia's victory not only incited the fans, but made Faarooq jealous. A struggle ensued between Maivia and Faarooq for control of the Nation of Domination. It was a struggle Maivia refused to lose. While Faarooq had been recruiting Ahmed Johnson, who turned out to be of little use for the Nation, Maivia had recruited Mark Henry, who was a far better selection for the group.

Maivia, however, wasn't interested in asking for power. He wasn't interested in taking a vote. There was no way he was going to sit down and work things out with Faarooq. He simply took what he wanted: more power. He actually had the nerve to volunteer Faarooq for a match against powerhouse Ken Shamrock.

"I've got the power because I've got the belt. What's he got?" Maivia asked. "He has a big mouth, but he doesn't have much else going for him. The Rock is the leader of this group. The Rock is the best Intercontinental champion in history. I've proven myself. The Nation of Domination is mine. The Rock is just better suited to being a leader. If Faarooq really thought about things, he'd realize he's better off taking a lesser role with the Nation."

Maivia had a lot of things on his mind, like Shamrock, a former competitor in the Ultimate Fighting Championship (UFC) organization. Shamrock was one extremely

Former UFC champion Ken Shamrock declares his intention to topple Maivia and take the WWF Intercontinental belt from him.

tough opponent, and he gave Maivia all he could handle in match after match. Most of those matches were won by Shamrock, although Maivia was able to retain the Intercontinental belt by getting himself disqualified. If Maivia was an egotist, then Shamrock was a madman.

Their most famous match took place at WrestleMania XIV on March 29, 1998, in Boston. It was by far the most violent match of the evening, and probably the most memorable, too. Shamrock clearly dominated the contest. First he used a belly-to-belly suplex on Maivia, then he forced him to submit to an anklelock, a submission hold that puts excruciating pressure on the victim's lower leg.

Maivia screamed out in pain. Shamrock released the hold. Other members of the Nation stormed the ring and attacked Shamrock, who boldly cleared the ring of his attackers. Enraged, Shamrock placed Maivia in another anklelock. Again, Maivia screamed out in pain. Faarooq walked to ringside, but refused to help Maivia. The referee ordered Shamrock to release the hold. Shamrock pulled it tighter. Sweat and blood poured down Maivia's face. Four referees tried to calm the enraged Shamrock, but they couldn't break the hold, and the truth quickly became evident: Shamrock was trying to cripple Maivia! Shamrock finally broke the hold, then proceeded to slam all four referees.

Maivia was not only in tremendous pain, but he had lost his prized title. Or so it seemed. Because of Shamrock's heinous actions after the match, the decision was reversed. The belt was returned to Maivia, who had to be taken away on a stretcher. Shamrock stormed down the runway, tipped over the stretcher, and slammed Maivia to the floor.

"I don't understand," Shamrock asked. "How can you reverse what's already done? You can't change history. I won!"

"There are certain sets of rules that everybody has to follow," Maivia responded, "and one of those rules is that if the referee calls for a break, you have to break. Shamrock ignored the rules. He was trying to break the Rock's leg."

Not only was Maivia winning his battle to retain the I-C title, he was also winning his battle for control of the Nation. Henry, Mustafa, and Brown were clearly on his side, and Faarooq had no choice but to accept a lesser role. Finally, the tension became too much for either side to stand, and Faarooq was booted out of the organization. His insubordination toward Maivia at WrestleMania had been the final straw.

Faarooq became the Nation's number one enemy. At the Unforgiven pay-per-view on

April 26, 1998, Faarooq teamed with Shamrock and Steve Blackman to defeat Maivia, Brown, and Henry. Despite the fact that he really didn't care what the fans thought about him, Maivia was actually becoming popular again. Not popular in the sense of approved and liked but popular in the tradition of "Stone Cold" Steve Austin. The Rock had an attitude, and people were entertained by it.

He used catch phrases such as, "Can you smell what the Rock is cookin'?" and "Know your role and shut your mouth." He started calling himself the "People's Champion." His signature finishing move, a bruising elbow, was called the "People's Elbow." He invited his opponents into the "Smackdown Hotel," where he'd "lay the smack down" on them, a euphemism for being beaten and defeated. Yet there was a difference between Rocky Maivia, the wrestler, and Duane Johnson, the man who became the Rock.

"There's a huge responsibility," he said of his position as a role model. "It's extremely important to me, outside of the ring, outside of the character, that these kids realize you have to go to school. It's the age-old story. You do have to go to school, get your grades, make sure your grades are up, and do the right thing. It's hard in this day and age to escape the peer pressure. But, believe me, look peer pressure straight in the face and tell those other guys who want you to do drugs or take pills or take crack or smoke or whatever it is, and say, 'Hey, I'm going to do the right thing.' It's just that simple."

Each time the Rock's signature music played and Maivia made his way to the ring, there were fewer and fewer boos and more and more cheers. Perhaps, for Maivia, it was a matter of knowing his own role and not caring what other people thought about him. Even a loss to Shamrock in the finals of the June 28, 1998, King of the Ring tournament didn't slow Maivia. He had a summer-long feud with Hunter Hearst Helmsley, and wasn't shy at all about messing with Chyna, Triple-H's powerful female bodyguard.

This was an unusual feud because Helmsley and Maivia were both considered rulebreakers. Prior to their match on July 4, 1998, in Vancouver, Canada, they insulted each other before getting down to the business of wrestling. Finally, after Maivia floored Triple-H with a DDT, Chyna grabbed Maivia's boot.

When the Rock and Triple-H vied for supremacy in the WWF during the summer of 1998, their unusual rule-breaker vs. rule-breaker feud included lots of interference from Helmsley's bodyguard Chyna, who helped Helmsley claim the I-C belt.

Helmsley tried to use his finishing move on Maivia, but D-Lo Brown and Mark Henry of the Nation interfered. Helmsley won by disqualification, but didn't get the belt.

Interference was the common denominator in the Maivia vs. Helmsley feud. The Nation would interfere on Maivia's behalf, while Chyna would interfere on Helmsley's behalf. Rarely was there a clean winner in any given match, but the Nation of Domination vs. D-Generation X was the feud of the summer.

Turmoil within the Nation was the side story that summer. On July 14, D-Lo Brown beat Helmsley for the European title after Maivia nailed Helmsley with his favorite move, the "Rock Bottom," a variation of the powerbomb. Maivia, however, was angry at Brown, because he felt he had to win the belt for him and, thus, the Nation.

The war between the Nation and D-Generation X reached its boiling point five days prior to SummerSlam '98. Owen Hart and Mark Henry held Chyna in the ring while the rest of D-Generation X was locked inside a dressing room. Maivia acted as if he was going to kiss Chyna, then turned away in disgust and ordered Henry to kiss her. Shawn Michaels of D-X stormed the ring and ran off the Nation.

The Triple-H vs. Maivia feud culminated at SummerSlam when they battled in front of a packed house at Madison Square Garden. It was a ladder match, in which the Intercontinental title belt was hung from a rope above a ladder set up in the middle of the ring. The winner—and champion—would be the first man to retrieve the belt. The match was grueling. The two hated rivals battered each other

Rulebreaker or not, the Rock takes his position as a role model seriously and tells his fans that they need to stay in school and say no to drugs.

with a sense of fury and ferociousness rare even for them. Both men used the ladder as a weapon, but it was Chyna's interference that turned out to be the difference. She struck Maivia with a low blow that knocked him off the ladder and allowed Triple-H to grab the belt and claim the Intercontinental championship.

Maivia was furious. He couldn't believe the WWF had allowed Chyna to interfere in such an important match. Maivia petitioned the federation for a one-on-one match against Chyna.

"The Rock has absolutely had it with that piece of trash," Maivia swore. "If the suits can't teach Chyna her role, then the Rock will do it."

The Rock was simply out of control. A one-on-one match against Chyna was just not going to happen. Had he lost his mind? Was he turning crazy? As summer turned to fall in 1998, the Rock was, in fact, ready to make another turn of his own.

THE ROCK SAYS . . .

In the fall of 1998, the WWF was in a state of turmoil. Although "Stone Cold" Steve Austin was the World champion, federation head Vince McMahon was determined to wrest the title from Austin by any means necessary, even if he had to cheat. Despite McMahon's best efforts, Austin was resilient.

After losing the Intercontinental title, Maivia decided he was more interested in winning his first WWF World title than in regaining the secondary belt. Maivia's head became swollen with success. He signed a new six-year contract with the WWF that would pay him a minimum of $400,000 a year. Whether this angered the other members of the Nation never became clear, but this much did: they started to think that the Rock was his own man, not the Nation's man.

At the Breakdown pay-per-view on September 27, Maivia squared off against Mankind and Ken Shamrock in a three-way match to decide the number-one contender to the WWF World title. To Maivia's surprise, the fans started chanting, "Rocky! Rocky!" and screaming epithets at Shamrock. Maivia didn't know what had prompted this change. He was confused. Maivia won the match, but that same night, the World title was held up because of another controversial three-way match involving Austin, The Undertaker, and Kane.

The Rock thought he had Stone Cold beat at WrestleMania XV, but Austin revived in time to escape Maivia's "corporate elbow" finisher and pin the Rock for the WWF World heavyweight title.

Two weeks later at *Monday Night Raw*, the Rock squared off against The Undertaker. Early in the match, Mark Henry and D-Lo Brown of the Nation appeared at ringside to cheer Maivia. Kane walked to The Undertaker's corner to protect his half-brother. When The Undertaker and Kane both went after Maivia, Brown and Henry left him to fend for himself.

Before long, the Nation became less and less influential. Maivia really didn't care. He had bigger things to worry about, like Vince McMahon. The Nation was yesterday's news.

At *Raw* one week, McMahon told Maivia that since he hates the people, he also hates the People's Champion: Maivia. McMahon began scheming against the Rock. He told him that if he didn't win the Intercontinental title from Shamrock, the recently crowned champion, he would be booted out of the tournament to pick a new WWF World champion. Shamrock lost the match by disqualification. Maivia didn't get the belt.

"You're out of the tournament," McMahon told Maivia.

At another *Raw*, McMahon told the Rock that he would be out of the WWF if he didn't pin Henry, his former Nation of Domination teammate, or force him to submit. Near the end, McMahon came out with Big Bossman, who tried to handcuff Rocky to the cornerpost. Maivia resisted, then used a finishing move called the DDT on Henry. Shane McMahon, Vince's son, ran into the ring and made the three-count, signaling Rocky's victory.

The WWF World title tournament was held at the 1998 Survivor Series on November 15 in St. Louis. There were 14 competitors, including

Maivia, who had been allowed back into the tournament. In the first round, the Rock needed only four seconds to pin Big Bossman. It wasn't much of a win. Bossman, one of McMahon's cronies, purposely laid down and allowed the Rock to win.

Now the fans were getting suspicious, but they were squarely on the Rock's side when he met Shamrock in the second round. Maivia advanced to the semifinals when he intercepted Big Bossman's nightstick and used it to help gain the pin on Shamrock. Bossman, however, had never intended for Shamrock to get the nightstick. He meant it for Maivia. In the semifinals, The Undertaker was disqualified against Maivia because Kane interfered.

Still, the setup between Maivia and McMahon wasn't obvious until the final round, when Maivia went up against Mankind. When Maivia locked Mankind in a sharpshooter leglock, McMahon, who was at ringside, immediately ordered the timekeeper to ring the bell, even though Mankind hadn't submitted. Maivia was WWF World champion. McMahon climbed into the ring and Maivia hugged his boss. The fans were absolutely stunned by the ruse; Maivia had been scheming with McMahon all along.

Austin was enraged. He charged the ring and attacked both Maivia and McMahon. Austin was the most popular man in the WWF, and that now made Maivia the least popular, or maybe the second least-popular, after McMahon. Of course, the Rock was long past caring about the fans.

Even those who hated Maivia couldn't understand how this could have happened.

Maivia had always been his own man. He had never sold out to anybody; he had been a rebel.

"What a joke," D-Lo Brown told *Pro Wrestling Illustrated* magazine. "I thought this guy wanted respect. What does this say for wrestling? This guy had been down so long after losing the Intercontinental title. He had worked so hard to prove himself to himself. He made it back, was the 'People's Champion.' I wonder if he's holding his head high now after getting a freebie title."

"THE CROCK!" read the headline on the cover of *Pro Wrestling Illustrated*. Maivia had become wrestling's least-respected man. Maivia didn't care. He was more famous than ever. He insisted that he didn't sell out, he had just done what he had to do in order to get ahead.

Maivia recreated himself. The People's Champion became the Corporate Champion. The People's Elbow became the Corporate Elbow. Not that he became any less charismatic. Prior to his showdown with Mankind, the Rock boasted that he had made a special reservation for Mankind "at the Smackdown Hotel, right at the corner of Know Your Role Boulevard and Jabroni Drive."

Love him or hate him, the fans simply couldn't stop watching.

Even with powerful friends in high places, the Rock couldn't make Mankind honor his reservation at the Smackdown Hotel. On December 29, Austin's interference enabled Mankind to beat Maivia for the WWF World title. "I'll make it up to you," McMahon promised Maivia, who was furious over the loss.

"As you stand in the middle of the Rock's ring with the Rock's WWF title, it makes him sick because you're not worthy of being the

World champion. Your entire outfit cost about eight cents," said the Rock. Mankind refused to be goaded into a rematch, though, until Maivia challenged him to an "I Quit" match at the upcoming Royal Rumble. Mankind accepted, and it was payback time for McMahon.

The Mankind vs. Maivia match started with the two men brawling at ringside. When the action returned to the ring, both men used the ring microphone as a weapon. Maivia brought a ladder into the ring and used it on Mankind, then tried to handcuff Mankind's hands behind his back. Mankind fought back. Maivia battered him with a chair.

"You'll have to kill me," Mankind told Maivia. But after the 10th chairshot, Maivia held a microphone to Mankind's mouth, and Mankind said, "I quit." The Rock was World champion once again.

"You see what happens when superior minds like those of the Rock and Mr. McMahon

As members of McMahon's Corporation, Paul Wight, known as The Giant, and the Rock had teamed up to battle Mankind, but their alliance was an uneasy one and before long, they were wrestling one another.

work together?" Maivia asked. "Not only did we outwrestle those jabronis, we outfoxed them, too."

Mankind insisted he had never quit. "Come on, fellas," Mankind said. "That was obviously a piped-in voice. Somehow they got me on tape saying those words. Mankind doesn't quit."

Mankind and Maivia met again in an empty arena at halftime of the 1998 Super Bowl. They fought up the steps, through the cafeteria, in several offices, and even in the loading dock area of the Tucson Convention Center in Arizona. Finally, Mankind used a forklift to lower beer kegs onto the Rock and score the pin. Once again, Mankind was the WWF World champion.

Mankind vs. the Rock was the hottest feud in wrestling, and it became hotter at the St. Valentine's Day Massacre pay-per-view, in which they battled to a draw when neither man could answer the referee's 10-count.

This was one of the most emotional feuds in wrestling history, so emotional that both men were easily goaded into doing things they didn't want to do. The next night at *Raw*, Maivia demanded a rematch. Mankind refused. Finally, the Rock insulted him into accepting a ladder match that night.

When the bell rang, the Rock choked Mankind with a television cable. Mankind responded by throwing the metal ring steps at him. Maivia reversed a piledriver into a "rock bottom," flattening the announcer's table. As both men climbed the ladder, a new wrestler appeared: Paul Wight, who had wrestled in WCW as The Giant. He was there to help the Rock. Wight chokeslammed Mankind off the ladder, and Maivia retrieved the belt.

Right away, there was friction between Wight and Maivia, even though they were both ostensibly in McMahon's Corporation.

Maivia and Wight pushed and shoved. Other members of the Corporation tried to break them up, but Maivia and Wight agreed to a match with Mankind as the referee. It was another ruse. Maivia and Wight both attacked Mankind, then McMahon climbed into the ring and raised their hands.

But the Rock really did mistrust Wight, and claimed that Wight was aligned with Austin. McMahon warned the Rock not to air the Corporation's dirty laundry in public and assured him that Wight was a member of the Corporation.

The Rock and Wight finally squared off at the March 14, 1999, edition of *Sunday Night Heat*. When Wight went for a chokeslam, Mankind entered the ring with a chair and went after Wight. Austin then walked out and suggested that he might have an alliance with Wight. The next night, it became clear that Wight and Austin were on the same side, but McMahon wasn't happy with Maivia.

"This 'Rock' stuff is going to your head," McMahon told him. "You need a reality check, Duane. Look at who you have become and who you owe. What about everything my dad did for your grandfather, the 'High Chief' Peter Maivia?"

The main event for WrestleMania XV was Austin vs. the Rock for the WWF World title, but the subplot was: who would referee the match? That would be decided in a match between Mankind and Wight. Mankind won the match, but he was so severely powerbombed by Wight that it seemed doubtful he'd be able to referee Austin vs. the Rock.

McMahon appointed himself the referee for the match. "Not so fast," said WWF commissioner Shawn Michaels, who appointed Tim White referee for the match, which was as violent and exciting as expected. With nearly 13 minutes gone, Austin fought his way out of a chinlock. The Rock scored with a Samoan drop and covered Austin for the pin attempt. White only counted to two. The Rock, enraged over not getting the three-count, executed his "rock bottom" on the referee. Austin used his Stone Cold stunner on the Rock. Substitute referee Earl Hebner rushed to the ring and made a two-count.

Then Vince McMahon showed up at ringside. As the Rock and McMahon double-teamed Austin, Mankind came to the ring and attacked McMahon. Austin went for a pin on the Rock, and Mankind took over as referee and made a two-count. The Rock connected with a clothesline, then with his "rock bottom" once again. He was in position to win the match. Austin was laid out on the mat, but the Rock took too much time. He posed. He gloated. He came off the rope for his "corporate elbow," and Austin moved out of the way.

The Rock crashed to the mat, after which Austin executed his "stone-cold stunner." A three-count later, Austin was the new WWF World champion.

Ata Johnson, Rocky's mother, and Dany Johnson, his wife, were seated in the front row behind the broadcasters' table when Rocky lost the belt. "He's still my boy," Ata wept. "He's still my champion."

Maybe so, but his mother's and wife's love were all the Rock had left. His list of enemies was getting longer by the day. Austin defeated him in one rematch after another. Wight, who had choke-slammed McMahon at WrestleMania, beat him, too. Mankind was an enemy. Shane McMahon served as guest referee at the Backlash pay-per-view, but the Rock still lost to Austin.

With the Corporation on the verge of turmoil, Shane McMahon did the unthinkable: he fired the Rock for his losses to Austin. Suddenly, unthinkably, the Rock was on the same side as Austin and Mankind.

The Rock went on winning his matches, but they were against Big Bossman and other members of the Corporation. When he finally did get a match against WWF World champion The Undertaker at the King of the Ring in June 1999, he was pinned. A month later at Fully Loaded, he lost to Corporation member Hunter Hearst Helmsley in a falls-count-anywhere strap match. The Rock and Mankind formed an alliance and won the WWF World tag team title, but they lost the belts quickly to The Undertaker and Paul Wight. The Rock and Mankind twice regained the belts again, then lost them again.

The Rock's attempts at regaining the World title were also thwarted, but that didn't diminish his popularity with the fans, who loved him once again. They made his autobiography, *The Rock Says . . .* shoot to number one on the bestseller list.

As wrestling entered a new millennium, the list of wrestlers who will lead the sport's charge into the future was headed by a former football player, a third-generation wrestler named Rocky Maivia, the Rock.

Chronology

1972   Born Duane Johnson on May 2

1991   Starts his college football career with the University of Miami

1996   Makes his wrestling debut in the USWA as Flex Kavana; teams with Buzz Sawyer to beat Brickhouse Brown and Reggie B. Fine in the finals of a tournament for the vacant USWA tag team championship; loses the USWA tag team title, and regains it one more time; signs with the WWF and takes on the name Rocky Maivia; makes his WWF debut at the Survivor Series and wins an eight-man tag team match

1997   Wins the WWF Intercontinental title on February 13 from Hunter Hearst Helmsley; defeats former WWF World champion Bret Hart by disqualification; loses the Intercontinental title on April 28 to Owen Hart; joins the rulebreaking Nation of Domination; Steve Austin forfeits the Intercontinental title to Maivia on December 8

1998   Wrests control of the Nation of Domination from Faarooq; loses the Intercontinental title at SummerSlam to Hunter Hearst Helmsley; wins the WWF World heavyweight title at Survivor Series by beating Mankind in a tournament final; joins Vince McMahon's Corporation; loses the WWF World heavyweight title on December 29 to Mankind

1999   Regains the WWF World heavyweight title from Mankind at the Royal Rumble; loses the WWF World title at halftime of the Super Bowl to Mankind; regains the World title from Mankind at the St. Valentine's Day Massacre; loses the WWF World title at WrestleMania XV to Steve Austin; teams with Mankind to win the WWF World tag team title

2000   Autobiography *The Rock Says...* goes to number one on the best-seller list

2001   Makes his big-screen debut as the Scorpion King in *The Mummy Returns*; starts filming on *The Scorpion King*, a prequel to *The Mummy Returns*

Further Reading

Ethier, Bryan. "The Rock: What Makes You Love/Hate This Man?" *Inside Wrestling* (December 1999): 34–37.

Hunter, Matt. *Superstars of Men's Pro Wrestling*. Philadelphia: Chelsea House Publishers, 1998.

Mudge, Jacqueline. *Bret Hart: The Story of the Wrestler They Call "The Hitman."* Philadelphia: Chelsea House Publishers, 2000.

"Press Conference: The Rock." *Pro Wrestling Illustrated* (September 1999): 22–23, 58–59.

"Q&A: Rocky Maivia." *The Wrestler* (April 1998): 20–23.

"Rocky Maivia: Smacked Down and Fighting Back," *The Wrestler Presents True Life Stories* (Winter 1998): 16–25.

Ross, Dan. *Steve Austin: The Story of the Wrestler They Call "Stone Cold."* Philadelphia: Chelsea House Publishers, 2000.

Varsallone, Jim. "This Ain't No Sing Along: the Rock Rises to the Top of the Sports Entertainment Business." *WOW Magazine* (July 1999): 12–26.

Index

Photo Credits

Jeff Eisenberg Sports Photography: pp. 6, 14, 16, 19, 22, 25, 28, 30, 34, 36, 43, 46, 48, 60; David Fitzgerald: pp. 26; Sports Action: pp. 2, 8, 11, 38, 50, 55.

DAN ROSS has spent the last 10 years observing and writing about professional wrestling. His writing on wrestling, basketball, and baseball has appeared in numerous publications around the world, and he is a frequent guest whenever European radio and television stations require an American viewpoint on wrestling. He lives in upstate New York with his wife, son, and dog, and likes to brag to neighbors about the wrestling ring in his basement. His previously published volumes on the mat sport include *The Story of the Wrestler They Call "The Undertaker"* and *Steve Austin: The Story of the Wrestler They Call "Stone Cold."*

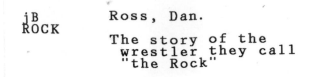

jB
ROCK

Ross, Dan.

The story of the
wrestler they call
"the Rock"

$19.75

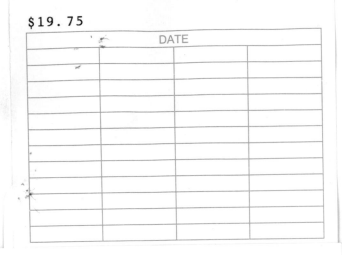

	DATE		